MEMORY KEEPER

MEMORY KEEPER

POEMS BY

APRIL TIERNEY

WAYFARER BOOKS
BERKSHIRE MOUNTAINS, MASSACHUSETTS

WAYFARER BOOKS

WWW.WAYFARERBOOKS.ORG

© 2022 TEXT BY APRIL TIERNEY

Quantity sales. Special discounts are available on quantity purchases
by corporations, associations, bookstores, and others. For details, contact the
publisher or visit wholesalers such as Ingram or Baker & Taylor.

All Rights Reserved
Published in 2022 by Wayfarer Books
Cover Design and Interior Design by Leslie M. Browning
Cover Image © Patrimonio
ISBN 978-1-956368-06-2
First Edition Trade Paperback

10 9 8 7 6 5 4 3 2 1

Look for our titles in paperback, ebook, and audiobook wherever books are sold.
Wholesale offerings for retailers available through Ingram.

Wayfarer Books is committed to ecological stewardship.
We greatly value the natural environment and invest in
environmental conservation. For each book purchased in our
online store we plant one tree.

CONTENTS

About the Author
About the Press

For Sloane

BURRS IN YOUR HEART

One morning, after a hike up the mythical mountain
that looks out over our home, I sit on the deck
picking burrs out of my socks—

it's late July and the grasses are going to seed,
which means they are enacting that brilliant,
evolutionary ritual of sending their offspring
along in my clothes to propagate this land
far and wide with their future exultation—

when a memory pierces my heart
just like those little, gold spears now
being carried off by the wind.

It's a memory of the time I listened
to a Hinóno'éí elder and master storyteller
weave magic into the world. She talked
about the childhood pain of being forbidden
to speak her native language at school,

and so lost it
at too ripe an age.
Which meant she also lost
the ability to converse
with her grandmother
at the end of her life.

She told stories about Thanksgiving,
and how perplexed her people were
that a single day in all of the year
should be reserved for gratitude,
when they began each morning this way.
So her family had no problem with gathering
for the holiday, although it was no different
than any other time of giving ordinary thanks.

She spoke about speaking,
and how she could go on forever.
How her community would gather round
to listen to her tell stories, but would always
bring food to whet the appetite of her tongue first;
fragrant soups with hominy, thick fry bread,
and sweetened tea. Only after bellies had been filled
would she begin to weave the evening's tale—
no one stirring until many hours later,
after the dark web of night carried her
mighty words off into the dreaming.

I sensed then that she was only getting started,
that I would sit there and listen forever. But the door opened
and one of the organizers of this lecture series abruptly
entered the room to inform the proud and silver haired
storyteller that her hour had come to its end. The burr
that is stuck in my body—just like those grass seedlings

in my socks—is what happened to her strong face
just then; the way it winced with five hundred years

of disrespect. The embodied memory (which was not in the past,
but a thing coiled up beside us then) of her people being cut off,
brutalized, massacred, and displaced. Most everyone else
in that room orderly packed up their bags and rushed off
to the next timed and terribly important thing, but I
could not move, nor could the Hinóno'éí woman,
with a thousand more important things to say.

Eventually the organizer pressed, and a new flock
of eager consumers began flooding through
the opened door. They needed this room
for someone else, and I do not
remember the rest.

Boulder, Colorado is the original winter homeland of the Arapaho People, whose name for themselves is Hinóno'éí. They were forced out of the area in 1859 when miners discovered gold in the foothills. The Southern Arapaho were sent to a reservation in Oklahoma, and the Northern Arapaho to Wyoming.

MAKING REAL

Sometimes the idea of something
is more real than the thing itself.

We waste our days, so our lives become
the wasted limbs of our longing.

Pure arrogance is to assume
that we will always be here;

but if breath was no longer an abstraction,
would you continue to sleep through
every sunrise? Or ignore the blue jays
returning in spring to sing the world alive?

Our dead are always conferring
their hunger upon us;

so I bake sweet things
that plump up fat and fragrant,

I give offerings—

all to make more real
this procession in time.

MY GRANDMOTHER IS THE WIND

She isn't *like* those great gusts
tearing through the trees, nor
is the trumpeting flight of air
somewhat *similar* to her.

This is no balmy metaphor,
my grandmother *is* the wind—

a feisty woman from Brooklyn
who never, in all of her eighty-four
years of living, learned how to drive a car.

She was born to parents
who carried the memory of salt
and sea breeze over from Poland
in the carefully packed compartment
of their sorely uprooted cells;

eventually passing along those briny drafts
to their golden haired daughter, aptly naming her
Shirley Schneider, who later would become Shirley Glaser—
a novice sculptor and painter of pottery, epic storyteller,
mother of two giants, and embodiment of the wind.

But her claim to fame was her mean roast chicken,
made so flavorful in her own oven, that she would

bake the bird in New York City, then freeze and pack it
snugly into her suitcase for the long flight out to Colorado.
The chicken would be properly defrosted by the time
she and my grandfather arrived, so we would
drive straight home to eat it. No sides or silverware,
only this delicacy placed in the center of our small table
as we gathered round to pluck at the flesh that my proud
grandmother had brooded over on our behalf. Then,
there was the perfectly sweetened honey cake served
in her crowded home during the High Holy Days,
which the rest of our family would hunger after
all year long. And she always mixed together
matzo brei with her remarkably misshapen hands,

working her arthritic knuckles into the
eggs and brittle, unleavened bread—
never using a spoon; never dreaming
of keeping her sweat, love, and pain
from anyone in her kitchen (it all
went into our breakfast too).

Sometimes my grandmother howls at night
and I lie awake to listen. She tells stories
of being pushed around in a baby stroller
by her mother—under blankets and alongside
bottles of bootleg gin during the time of prohibition;

during a time when my great grandmother made moonshine
in her bathtub and would stand atop a real soapbox
on the Brighton Beach Boardwalk to publicly scorn
the debauchery of American democracy.

Sometimes, during the middle of the day
I can feel my grandmother laughing;
she shakes the carpet of the Earth with her
deep throated cackle, offering all of the leaves
on the trees a good hard rattle. And
it's on those days that I watch her dance
too, like she loved to do with my grandfather

(who *is* the sun, which is
another story for another time).
That is, before her knees
and hips eventually gave way
to the tremendous pain
that her noble joints nurtured
through centuries of persecution.

But even then, when she was no longer able
to stand without wailing, if music came into the room
my grandmother would sit a little taller in her chair
and give her arms over to the air—hands flicking
this way and that, making a point to show life
that she was still intensely grateful to be granted

another day. So on this afternoon, when the wind

is especially spirited, I throw my arms up too;

we laugh, howl, and dance in concert

with all of the other strong, vocal ones

who bear the blessings of our

ancestral ways.

IN LOVE WITH THE WORLD

I was always in such a hurry,
but you taught me how
to slow down.

Our walks were more like meanders;
you would pause before any flower,
bending down to bury your slender nose
into their sweetened petals.

And each little cup of gold or lavender
would hold onto your lovely face;
they would keep you there,
whispering secrets into your soul.

You would squeal with delight,
swooning over their delicate
fragrance and lavish colors.
They often blushed in return.

I watched you—
so in love with the world—
daydreaming about the day
when I might fall, too.

INTERSPECIES MUSIC MAKING

Last night during the middle of dinner,
a cricket cast out his lofty song from the top
of our twelve foot high, dust lacquered rafters.

How does so tiny a creature
make such an enormous sound,
we pondered? How did he
get inside, and jump up so high?

After exploring all possibilities—
including taking out the ladder
and calling up to the ceiling,
asking our longwinded friend
if he would like to rejoin
the rest of his ensemble
outside in the dark
husk of night—

my husband
did the only
reasonable thing
a man could do,

the only proper response
to anyone singing their hearts out
in the middle of your kitchen.

He got out his guitar and together
they made music like nothing
I have ever heard before, or since.

They played until the cricket's
voice became sore and in need of rest;
until my husband's strong fingers
throbbed and threatened to bleed.
By then, I was wholly drunk
on wonder and sleep.

BEARING WITNESS

Twice now I have watched giant snakes
feasting upon other families' babies.
The first time was in the woods,
winding down a rough trail with a friend—
we heard the birds screeching well before
we spotted their devastation; dozens
of little chickadees bouncing around
in the trees, crying out in maddening screams

truly as if their lives and their offspring's
depended upon it. Then we saw
the wide body of a snake
wrapped halfway up and around
the trunk of an enormous tree

which had a hollow right at its center—
as if the tree's mouth had been caught
mid-scream too. The snake's head
was deep in that hollow, and as the clan
of birds bounced from limb to limb in a torrent
of commotion, my friend and I stood with jaws
dropped to the forest floor watching
the snake slowly ingesting then digesting
golfball size clumps like a conveyer belt
down her smooth, elongated body.

The baby birds seemed to remain intact
as they traveled through that dark tunnel
into the opened arms of their death.
Such a chilling, unforgettable sight.

A woman and man stumbled up the trail
just then. The woman let out a yelp,
"This is awful! We must stop it!
Quick," she said to the man beside her,
"throw a stick at the snake!" But he
just stood there, staring; surely stilled
by the rare grandeur of it all.

I wondered if anyone had ever yelled
at her mid-lunch, "No! Stop! Don't
you dare take in another bite!"
Of course not. What respectable person
would try to stop life from exquisitely
living? Isn't death the only way
any of us go on existing?

~

The second encounter was halfway
below the rim of the Grand Canyon.

I was resting in the shade with a few
friends and my shoes kicked off
when a rattlesnake casually
slid past the place we were sitting—

directly over my hiking boots and into
the dense grass. My friend jumped up
onto the picnic table and I scooted back
as we watched a ground squirrel barrel up to
the rattler, then toss sticks in his direction.
Meanwhile, another squirrel started yelling
at the first one from high up in a tree,
pleading with his love to move back.
But she would not. She kept screeching

and tossing up Earth; the fiercely
protective mama that she was,
desperately trying to defend her nest.
The snake seemed unfazed by this, slowly
coiling himself up and around her babies;
his head tucked into the center of his lap,
quietly feasting on those little, furry lives.

This time, I could not see the tunnel body
slowly digesting in his well-contained coil,
but surely felt sorrow and astonishment
working its way through my own simple flesh.

The squirrel in the tree kept beseeching
his sweetheart on the ground to back down
while she carried on with the agony of it all.

We sat there for what seemed like hours
until finally the snake slithered off
leaving no trace of the nest in his wake.
The squirrels eventually stopped screaming
and the silence that echoed off the walls
of the canyon will live on in me forever.

THE RIGHT KIND OF QUESTION

So often we are taught to ask
the wrong kinds of questions—

scratching our heads,
silently thinking

of all the things we want
from this bountiful life.

Instead, we should be shouting
into the unmarred air, "Life,
what do *you* want from me!?"

Then, spend the rest of our days
with heads bent to the wind,

listening.

The right kind of question
labors on Mystery's behalf;

its purpose is to praise
rather than plunder

all the unseen futures

of our collective
imagination.

MORNING PRAYERS

Every day in autumn, my husband wakes before dawn
while I continue laying in our soft bed listening to him
getting dressed in the dark. His movements are
monastic—all adorned in prayer and devotion.

There is purpose to the way he pulls on his pants
and hunting jacket; quietly, so as to not disturb
his adoring wife (who has grown accustomed
to waiting for the sound of the alarm—laying
awake for some time, though rarely lets on).

I hear the front door open, then close,
and feel his sturdy body walking
up the steep hill behind our house;
his footsteps slowly settle me
back into the dreaming.

Each morning he sits under the same pine tree,
where he remains for at least a few hours—
well past sunrise and the frost's first radiant glow.

He watches the deer as they greet the day;
combing the stilled landscape in their small
families, heads bent in gratitude over what little
green grass remains. He tracks their stealth frames,
learns their patterns, admires their power and grace.

His rifle is always at his side, and more often than not
these curious, four-legged kin come close enough
to stare (perhaps even as an offering to this honorable
hunter and the family he is beholden to). But more often still,
my husband is held in place by their proximity and
inexplicable beauty; and so, he does not take the shot.

A mama with her two fawns visits often;
the little ones mewing at him, surely by now
recognizing this equally mysterious man
sitting in the morning light. When he comes in—
often frozen to the bone as I am folded over
a hot breakfast—he laments at not being able
to lift his gun, at how much he hates the killing.

"The does remind me too much of you," he says,
always with a soft flame in his eyes. He admits
that all he is capable of out there is prayer.

And then the morning comes when I hear the shot.
It is so loud, it billows throughout my whole body.
I instantly know that some gorgeous deer has died
as I open my eyes to the blazing orange sun
lifting his sleepy head above the horizon. So I too
begin to pray. Then my good man comes in to get me.

"Quick. Get dressed. I need your help."
His posture is reverent, humble, grief-stricken.
So I dress and follow him up the mountain,
bringing local maize and sage to offer this one
who has offered her life to us, and the tiny,
growing babe that I now carry in my womb.

She is so newly dead, she appears nearly alive—
laying on her side, still steaming with warmth.
Her eyes are open and pink tongue hangs
from her mouth, tasting the early rays
that sweep out across the morning.

We kneel and speak aloud our gratitude,
admiration, blessings, and heartbreak;
laying beauty on the ground beside her.
Then together, we slowly carry this great one
down the mountain. I hum as we walk, holding
her elegant hooves in our trembling hands.

This doe, who in my husband's eyes,
looks so much like me, surely is a part of our
family; surely will nourish our bodies
and go on breathing with our storied beings.
We vow to live well into her good name.

HOW THINGS ARE

Stretch your little heart past
the familiar fields of adolescence,

become something the Gods can be proud of—
not heroic and self-important, but humble

and honest. Become recognizable to the fox
and falcon; the snowflakes falling at midnight.

Tear down that shrine you built
for how things should forever be,

and stand naked
in what they are.

WEAVING THE WORLD

In European folk traditions, it is said
that there are always women weaving

in each village and
at every hour of the day
and night,

for they are the ones
who weave the world
into existence.

These days, I often think about
all the hands that sit idle—

painfully replaced by
automation and inertia—

and I suspect it is true,
that life has withered
at the hem of modernity.

So to make anything,
to lean over a loom
or piece of wood,

is to declare a great love affair
with the beating heart
of creation.

MYTHIC DAYS

When the nurse nudged my pants down
and tucked a towel into the waist band
so as to not slop gel all over my clothes,
it felt strangely familiar, even though
this was my very first ultrasound.

When she began to unceremoniously move
the wand around my belly and make marks
on her black and white screen, somehow
I already knew the routine. Perhaps

my bones were tossing up the memory
of my mother stretched out on this same
butcher paper sheathed hospital bed—
though at that time, I would have been
the tiny baby bouncing around
on the mounted screen.

My mom already knew I was a female then,
long before the doctors would confirm it.
She'd been waiting for me for a long time;
taking her temperature every morning,
swearing by a small window each month
held purely for the composition of baby girls.

She even walked prayerful circles around
Sloan's Lake, a place that she knew
held power to bestow daughters
upon believing mothers. Everyone rolled
their eyes when she spoke of these things

saying she was silly; bearing too close a resemblance
to their own witchy ancestors, who were all burned
at the stake for upholding such irrational truths.

But back in this brightly lit hospital room,
I look at her grandbaby bouncing
up and down on the screen, with two
little hands and sweetly growing feet.
I am astonished, though not bewildered.

I have been a part of this ordeal before.
Two times in fact—once in my mom's
womb, and much earlier than that
in my grandma Bonnie's, safely tucked
into the tiny ovaries of my fetal mother.

All while my grandma also carried a secret thought,
something that women were forbidden to speak aloud
at the time—that she never wanted to become a mother.
Except this secret was impossible to keep from the cells

that she conferred upon her future daughter
and granddaughter. A thought, that decades later,
we both would need to free ourselves from.

So now, at thirty-four years old,
marveling at my husband's wide,
glistening eyes as he watches
our child light up the dark screen,

I wonder what this little one
will remember of our shared lives,
and how much more beauty
we can infuse into these
deeply mythic days.

BECOMING

Our futures unfold inside
these moments of becoming.

Do not back away,

you are kneeling
into the watershed

of all things
worth living.

No one ever promised
comfort along the path
to reclamation—

the old stories profess
dragons and dark forests
littered with doorways
to the Underworld.

Who would trade in
such epic tales
for a memoir

of leisure and convenience;
for a halfhearted shot
at belonging?

WHAT GOES AND WHAT STAYS BEHIND

There was a time, not too long ago,
when we fled from our home late at night

as three blazing fires claimed the forests
nearby. The sky was stiff with smoke,
for days I could not go outside.

News of the devouring flames
clawed through our community,
anxiety close behind.

Around ten o'clock on Saturday night,
just as orange and red arms began
to rise up from the distant hillside

causing a halo of light to lap out
across the land that we love,

my husband made the call to leave—
his first major decision as a father-
to-be. It was only three days

after learning about this little life
inside of my belly, and already
we were being acquainted
with displacement—

something our ancestors knew well
and were now sharing with us
so that one day we might know how to
fully embody our longing for home.

We quickly sifted through our things;
it's a human-making endeavor,
choosing what goes and what
stays behind. In the end

we brought nothing
of the practical kind,

nothing that could help us comfortably
start a new life. Our cars were piled high
with handwoven blankets and scarves,

pottery, books, locally crafted hats,
my loom and yarn, homemade baskets,
my man's guitar; things that would help us
locate our humanity again, if and when

we lost our way. We said goodbye to our house,
to those great wooden walls and furniture
that cradled our bodies through illness,

laughter, and love making. We sent our gratitude
up to the ceiling, maybe for the very last time,
and spoke our prayers deep into the night.

We hung a note on the front door for the firemen,
thanking them for their trouble, and laid Russian
sage around on the ground, pleading
with the Gods of our place for protection.

Then we drove down the mountain in the dark,
as flames licked the smoke-filled-sky and ceramic bowls
rattled an ancient tune in my front passenger seat.

ARTICLES OF FAITH

Fear is the founder of erosion.
It backs us into a voiceless corner,

one we never imagined
for ourselves, or others.

But language is the valley
through which we heal—

good lyrics are crafted there,
as are folktales and articles of faith.

Courage unveils the way
to sovereignty,

to unfounded fortune
forever made
to be given away.

DO YOU EVER THINK ABOUT THE DAYS

Do you ever think about the days
when the rain lavished kisses
all over your lonesome skin?

Or that time when the thick coat of winter
draped his arms around your quivering shoulders
and muttered promises of redemption?

What about when the hot summer sun
licked your bare back and sent
ripples of ravishment
all throughout your boiling blood?

Or when the wind came
to cool down that
insufferable yearning?

Do you ever reminisce about
the plush scent of the pine forest,
the one that held you gently
for such an honest stretch of time?

Or the sound of the waves
lapping up against the shore
as into the confluence
of your own careful heart?

No? Well then, at least
you can rest knowing

that they all
think about you.

HEAPING PORTIONS

I love the big dipper,
always have—

and not because it's the easiest
constellation to see in the sky,
but because of the immensity

of its ladle. I imagine such a vessel
plunging deep down into the
cook pot of our souls

to fish out all the best bits
from the very bottom
of that well,

then serving up heaping
portions of steaming
stories into every
wanting bowl.

It's a generosity of spirit
I can fully stand behind—

or in this case
beneath,

as the sky draws up
yet another

astonishing night.

THE MOST NATURAL THING IN THE WORLD

There was once a Deer Woman
who carried a little Lion Cub

inside the full moon
of her mythic womb.

Some said
it was a miracle;

others, the most natural
thing in the world.

HER VIOLATION

I once heard a poet speak about her sexual abuse
while her son was sitting in the audience
(I know this because she introduced him
as her pride and joy at the beginning of the show).

They were taking a summer road trip across the country
to promote her new book. I don't know how long
they had been on tour, or how many times he
had listened to her recite that devastating poem

but I watched his face as she delivered the lines,
describing each moment of her violation.
He never flinched or averted his eyes
from the stage. To think, twelve years old

and already a man. I wanted to put a hand on his back,
to hold him or rock him. I wondered if he cried
the first time he heard her story, the way I stumbled
from the store when it was all over; face wet,
hands trembling—wanting to change the world.

DEAR EUROPEAN DESCENDANTS

1.

Here's the truth of it:
things were bad where we came from.
If they were good, our people would not have left.

Persecution, disease, famine, displacement,
colonization disguised as religious salvation;

empire, slavery, witch burnings,
obliteration of vast wilderness—
who wants to remember any of it?

Which is why that journey across the sea
held the draw of amnesia; of leaving it all behind
and beginning anew. But let's be honest,

our pain followed us. Just because
you've stopped talking about
where you come from
or what happened there,
does not mean the past
has forgotten you.

2.

Who says our ancestors
are in the past, anyway?

Ghosts traveled with us on the ships
and departed at the same harbor.
We no longer speak their names

and long ago dispelled their languages,
but we are the embodiment of
their stories and prayers.

We are remembered into being
each time we open our eyes again
in the benevolent morning light.

There are people and lands
that we come from,
whether or not we choose
to claim them.

How could exile be free
from consequence?

3.

History does repeat itself,
even if you don't believe it.
Even if you are consumed
by the current headlines

and shake your finger in the face
of all that is wrong with the world;
especially if you position yourself
outside of what went wrong.

What is happening now
is shaped by the refusal
to acknowledge
what has been.

What difference does it make
that we should know who
and where we come from?

It makes all the difference
in the world.

INSATIABLE

I devour books.
I can't help myself.

One unsuspecting word
after another; inhaling
the pages so quickly,
sometimes I become
dizzy with beauty

and overwhelmed
by meaning.

I long for the language
that was not spoken
when I was younger,
that remained silent
as I got older.

I pursue what has been lost
in writing like a hunter,
whose hunger is not a luxury
and will not be satiated
by pleasantries.

Each lovely phrase,
every glint of truth—
always leaves me
breathless for more.

~

A poet I admire
once advised
in her prelude

against reading the book
cover to cover, but rather
one slow section at a time
before going to bed each night.

Even still, I proceeded to devour
the entire thing in one sitting—
picking my teeth at the end
like a lioness

utterly stuffed to the gills
with imagery and poetry.

~

Sometimes I can be
stalled by my curiosity

to know more about the
person behind the pen—
pausing mid-sentence

to research where they came from,
who their parents are, what impulses
drive them back, over and over again,
to the formidable, blank page.

~

Recently, it was a humble novel
that succeeded in slowing
down this insatiable hunger

simply by yoking my own
ancestral memories
into the spinal column
of the main characters'.

A Polish boy who escaped
the nazis after they barged
into his home and brutally
killed his kindhearted family.

He ran off into the woods,
and buried himself below
the Earth, so only his lips
and nose remained above
ground—kissing the sky,
supplicating upon life.

He dug his grave by day
and wandered the woods
looking for food by night.

I could only comprehend
these words in miniature gulps,
like drinking the swollen air
of that Polish nightmare
through a pin-sized straw.

I'd pause every few pages,
to feel my heart desperately
beating, then breaking.

To remember my cousin Isaac,
who is the only name or story
my family knows, though surely
there are more. How so many

fled into the forests
and bogs after everyone
around them had been killed
or taken away to the camps—
running to escape their fate.

But when you run from
what has been written, where
does the narrative end?

And who put those words down
onto the page to begin with?

The two exquisite books referenced here are
The Unwinding: and other dreamings by Jackie Morris
and Fugitive Pieces by Anne Michaels.

GUARDIANS OF THE DANCE

Sitting in the corner of that old ballet studio
as the pianist strums the heart strings
of every listening ear,

you look on—
not yet old enough
to understand heartbreak
but still alive in this world,

feeling the chords running through
your young body, sharp and true.

You were never cast in those roles;
the ones with the elaborate tutus,
with the swan whom the prince desired
and every other girl wanted to be.

Even still, you know the movements—
the way the ballad rises then steeply falls;
your body sung into youthfulness
at the fluttering feet of such passion
and grace. So maybe it's true,
what they say; that memory

is bestowed upon
an entire community.
That it is kept precious
by the dancing or watching
bodies of all who kneel
at the temple gates.

THE COST OF CONSUMPTION

One blazing summer afternoon,
I sat with a friend outside on her driveway;
sipping our iced drinks, wearing our brimmed hats,
and melting in the shade of her suburban home.

Crisp, green lawns (despite the three weeks of drought)
and oversized garbage bins neatly arranged on the curb
for trash day, all throbbed in the sweating sun.

My friend went inside to retrieve a snack
while I watched a woman drift along the sidewalk
with a big trash bag slung over her stooped shoulder.

She stopped in front of the neighbor's house
to rummage through their recycling bin,
put a few things in her sack,
then carried on in my direction.

She looked at the containers poised
on my friend's curb, then paused
when she spotted me
watching her.

Like any proud woman, she raised her chin
and we smiled at one another; her
leathery face showing its exhaustion.

She hesitated, then decided to pass by
the looming bins between us, carrying her dignity
along with that hefty bag over her now lifted shoulder—
only to stop once again in front of the next house,
bending over into their wide pail of waste.

How much money could this woman possibly make
by gathering what others had thrown away?
I know that in Cambodia, there are orphans

who live in the garbage dumps,
receiving less than a dollar a day
for collecting bottles and cans
buried beneath the walls of
wreckage and rot.

I know this because I was there; twenty-two
and wholly naive to the desolation of the world.
I saw children combing through mountains of trash
or huddled together atop the steaming heaps
in their battered tent homes, struggling to stay alive.

There was one little boy no older than three,
who was sitting alone, sucking on a broken bottle;
his sister was a few mounds away with her back
bent over their gray world, working.

I approached these two and knelt down,
trying to lull the jagged glass out of his mouth,
offering my arms for comfort instead.

He climbed in and I held his tiny,
beating heart against my aching chest
as stench rose and tears overwhelmed my eyes.
Tell me, who can defend the cost of consumption
against so many undeserving lives?

A TRUTHFUL WORLD

If you could have a secret language
inscribed all over your bare-skinned body,
what creature of beauty would it be?

I would elicit the wavering words
of baby cows, all glistening and resolute
in the muffled fields of late winter;

all curled up in tiny heaps
atop the frozen Earth,
pressing their soft bellies
onto a dreaming world.

We have three new calves in our neighborhood,
and another on the way—its white-faced mama
stands apart from the others, all enormous and miserable;
I can certainly relate. I wonder what it would be like
to behold her giving birth, the way my neighbor
watched in awe as another from the herd licked
the placenta off her newly dropped babe.

I walked over to the fields as soon as I caught word,
wanting to welcome this dewy life into our backcountry
community. Her legs were wobbly, but sure enough
she was already walking; bleating for milk,
bloody umbilical cord still dangling.

Her mother would not move closer to her,
standing among the sea of others,
allowing her newborn to bramble about.
The calf kept crying into that cold February air,

one unsteady step after another.
At only a few hours old, this babe
was being taught how to navigate
her way through a truthful world.

I inched closer to the fence in amazement,
while placing a hand on the crest
of my overstretched coat, then pausing
to drag in a manure-filled breath.

"Welcome to the world little one," I bellowed,
feeling my own baby squirming around in my belly.
"If this child is blessed enough to make it here too,
I pray they are as brave and beautiful as you."

FALLING INTO REMEMBRANCE

There are ruins
unmoored in our minds.

We relive exile,
ours and others.

In the Jewish tradition,
the act of forgetting
is held in high regard

as it means you get to fall
over and again

into remembrance.

And doesn't everything bear
the face of the Beloved?

I often forget what it feels like to be held
by the living roots of the Earth,
which is why I commonly visit
a circle of Elder Trees

to lay this needful body
where the deer have
bedded down.

So where do you go
to call your bones back

from their fortress
of forgetfulness?

WILDERNESS OF GRIEF

When news fanned out about the boy that I grew up with
overdosing on heroin as a thirty-seven year old man,

I immediately thought of the basketball games
and sleepovers—how you were best friends
with my older brother, for too short a time.

How our families loved one another,
while I was tormented by a crush
on your younger brother—a boy with a sweet,
round face, too shy to even speak to me.

I thought of the way our families split in high school
when you became too cool to spend time
with my lonely brother. Somehow,
I got invited to those same cool parties
at too young an age. I lied to my mom

as a fourteen-year-old girl, drinking
at houses emptied of parents where
eighteen-year-old drunk and horned up boys
eyed me hungrily from across the kitchen.

It's true, your presence there protected me.
You must have remembered my childhood room
full of stuffed animals and innocence, as you kept watch
over the famished boys with your tall, looming frame.

When my mom caught wind of the lie
and tracked me down that late winter night,
arriving at some oversized house
in her pajamas and sleep-rattled hair,
you were the one who answered the door.

You helped her find me in the sea of swirling bodies,
and she forgot her long-held frustration at you
for abandoning her only son so many years before;
a small price to pay for safeguarding her daughter now.

I have not thought of you in a very long time,
but today I remember your once admired name.
I wonder how your family is facing their wilderness
of grief, and if your soul will be troubled forever.

STORYLINES

Can you recall a time when
the Earth ripped herself in two
to birth the storyline of your life?

Can you conjure up the image of your Old Ones
gathered round your birthplace, conferring
every God-filled word and face of the cosmos
upon your jawline, thumbnail, artisanal spine?

Can you evoke a time when you were not this small,
isolated thing tumbling about a militant world
with no Mother Tongue to call your own?

When you were ennobled by the truth
of a lineage you could be proud of—
one you could hold up in your hands
amidst the shimmering light, and sing.

ANCIENT WISDOM

I once watched baby sea turtles
on a beach in Costa Rica
hatch from their bejeweled eggs
and make that mighty pilgrimage
toward the holy waters of the sea.

My husband and I stood in awe
as hundreds rose up from the beach,
like little half-dollars shining
in the silver moonlight.

They immediately knew which direction
to face—an ancient wisdom sewn into the
structure of their sand strewn bodies.
What would have taken me mere minutes
to walk to the water, required hours from them;

but no human hand can help herald
these brave beings along, for it is said
that then they would not know how
to return to the same shoreline

to lay their own eggs
into the fertile belly
of the Earth.

And how do they find their way back
to this very place of their birth,
after twenty to thirty years
of swimming in the vast ocean?
Pure ancestral magic.

So we threw our hands up into the evening air,
waving away a flock of hovering gulls
and encouraging those tiny hatchlings,
aimed like pointed arrows, toward Mother Sea.

SILENCES

As a child, I had a reoccurring nightmare
where everyone I knew drowned in a flood.
I was at my best friend Annie's birthday party
which was a picnic at a park with balloons
and a gorgeous cake on cloth covered tables.
The sun was shining, the birds were singing.

Suddenly, a torrent of water engulfed this
peaceful scene and everything turned dark.
I watched as all of my family and friends
were carried off by the deluge. Somehow,
I was the only one who could see or breathe
underwater, so I desperately tried to save them—
swimming in that fierce current, which became
the whole wide world. I soon realized
my efforts were hopeless, as I floated alone
in that underwater place, numbness all around.

Eventually, I came upon a man whose head had been cut off
and he was holding it in his hands. This is the moment
when I would always wake up—eyes wide, panting
into my dark room at night; and yet, I never told my parents.
Perhaps I believed that if I spoke the nightmare aloud
it would all come true. So I kept my silences
to protect them, and remained haunted
by this same scene for several years.

I've thought about the headless man
throughout my life; even seeing him a few times
in the waking world—my mom's second
and third husbands, many politicians.

But mainly, I am afflicted by
all the things we each quietly bear,
since my silences failed to save anyone.
My mom still drowned in the slowly
filling lobes of her ailing lungs,
even if it was a few decades later.

———

For Audre Lorde and her brilliant essay,
The Transformation of Silence into Language and Action

NIGHTHAWKS

Anger is a teacher,
so let her teach you.

Let her point out all of the places
where you abandoned your sincerity
along the side of the road

simply to appease
someone else—

where you stopped following
that great arch of your mythic life.

Let her show you where you have
held yourself silent when the world

needed you to speak;
where your fierce wisdom
was cut off at the knees.

Our shadows have grown so grotesque,
we've mistaken them for culture,

but now is the time to re-member
what has been deliberately suppressed;
to prepare a grand feast for all the
ghosts who've been starved by neglect.

Do not apologize when feathers fall
like nighthawks from your fiery eyes.

THE ANTHROPOCENE

My husband loves deciduous trees, which is to say
he loves the decadent foliage of undomesticated life.
He often aches for the east coast forests of his youth,

lamenting the absence of birch, oak, and maple in our pine-laden
home. But there is one patch of cottonwoods in which he relishes,
growing old and gnarly just down gulch from where we live.

They surround a small, seasonal pond where the frogs gather
to compose their springtime love songs. And we can see their twisted
branches reaching sunward from our deck—blossoming into bright,
heart-shaped leaves come May, then going out with a flame
in the fall amidst a sea of deep, coniferous green.

This morning I walked the winding path that encircles our five mile,
mountainous community with Lauren; a friend, fellow neighbor, and
wildlife biologist. As we approached the house that sits near the pond,
she informed me that someone had recently bought it after a long vacancy.
We heard the chainsaws before we saw the massacre, rounding the corner
upon two men in a whirl of destruction. Most all of the cottonwoods
had been severed at their ankles—trunks stacked in enormous heaps
around the snow covered cavern of the now-emptied pond.

We stopped to introduce ourselves and ask the men
what they were doing. Our new neighbor was forthright
in disclosing his plans for the place, that he and his wife

would be moving in three weeks, and much work was required
before then. "Most of these trees look dead anyway," he announced,
with no acknowledgment of the winter season we were all plainly
standing in. "Not to mention they need a ton of water—five hundred
gallons a day is what I read on the internet. Seeing as we would like
to get this pond going year round, that's just too much moisture
for a bunch of cottonwoods to be sucking up. So, they have to go."
I wanted to ask how much water he imagined taking from the ground
after drilling his well; if he thought it might be of equal proportions?
But instead, Lauren pointed out a bird singing in one of the
few trees left standing. "Do you hear that," she asked?

"No," he confessed. "It's a black-capped chickadee," she said.
"They depend upon this habitat for their nesting. Please
leave at least a few trees so they will have a place to go."
The conversation turned as the heat from their chainsaws cooled;
they seemed anxious to get back to what they were doing.

"Well, I heard they also attract tons of rattlesnakes,"
our new neighbor replied, while his friend remained silent.
"Our grandchildren will be playing around here and I want
to keep them safe," he nodded at me, looking for reassurance.
I admitted to seeing a few rattlers, though not many. Each time they've
warned me of their presence, and so I have thankfully stepped aside.
Why should we humans be the only ones to wander along the forest?

He ended by proudly telling us about how much his wife loves plants,
and that they would be growing several exotic species inside the house.
The irony—while standing in that boneyard—was too much to bear.

Lauren and I slunk home, heartbroken by what we had witnessed.
A flurry erupted in the neighborhood, people reaching out to one another
to share the news of these Old Ones being cut down—
they are neighbors just as much as any of us.

My husband stayed on the phone for a long while;
commiserating with our community, questioning permits,
acting upon his love for this singular riparian grove,
which has kept his sense of belonging alive
in a landscape so foreign from his original home.

Meanwhile, Lauren made the decision to go back over;
knocking on the door, having an honest conversation
with this amicable, yet oblivious man. She told him
how these trees are loved by so many, human
and more-than; how red tailed-hawks and
saw-whet owls would come to visit
if he left the rest standing.

Maybe some part of him softened around his ideas of this place,
and for a single glistening moment, could see the land as it truly was;
how it might be a worthy endeavor to learn to live alongside
the ones who have survived here far longer than we have,
instead of imposing ignorance upon an already intelligent
ecosystem. Whatever it was, he promised Lauren he would
stop cutting, and I have not heard the chainsaw since.

WASTED

I love the thesaurus—
although, I'm not proud to admit
that the one I routinely employ
is through dictionary.com

(my reliance on the territory
of untrammeled synonyms
is far too disorganized
for the sensuous use
of homebound text).

But, what I really mean to say
is that recently I looked up 'waste'
in this virtual sea of words,
and do you know what is given
as one of the genuine definitions?

Land that is uncultivated.

Under its subtitle lies:
bog, bush, desert, marsh,
jungle, tundra, and wilderness.

How could it be possible that land
must be touched by human hands
in order to be considered valuable?

I guess I can see it (though rather reluctantly)
through the lens of an industrialized society;
but from the perspective of someone
who is in a reciprocal relationship with this
seasonal, silky, sap-infused world,
it is utter rubbish—a proper synonym.

So I write a letter to the curators of this site,
listing all of the places which fall under
this particular characterization of waste,
then point out the richness that they bestow
upon our lives. I have yet to receive a response.

FAMILIAL GROUNDS

There is a trail my family used to visit
when I was young, on the way to or from
our favorite mountain hot spring—
just as my mom did when she was a little girl
with her father and two brothers.
It's a steep path carved far back into the
towering walls of a gorgeous canyon
with the Colorado River roaring below.

It was always quiet with ample parking,
so we would pack our lunches
and take our time climbing; passing
only a few people going up or coming down.
I remember each bridge we would cross
to traverse the trickles of water, and that old,
miniature log cabin where I fantasized about
making a life inside its mildewy walls.

I can still hear the laughter between me
and my brother, or the long-winded complaints
as our little lungs stretched themselves
into the thinning air; and the shaky ladder
towards the top, which only accentuated
our excitement. Then, finally summiting to see
that perfect, turquoise pool of water, shimmering
like gemstones in the alpine sun. It is a modest basin,

though she always greeted us kindly, recognizing
our familiar faces from seasons before.

An elegant waterfall trailed toward the back
that sometimes we would climb to, and the log
stretched out across the center, which occasionally
provoked challenges to be acted upon. But mainly,
we would eat our peanut butter and jelly sandwiches
while listening to the birds and water croon sweetly
into a royal blue sky. Maybe someone else would be
sitting at the water's edge too, but mostly not. Mostly,
we would bask alone as a family in that pure grace.

As I grew older, I stopped visiting the lake of my youth;
perhaps it was because my trips to the high country
became more sparse as my draw to the city mounted.
But at some point during that long absence, our
family trail got written up in a popular travel magazine
as one of the top things to do when visiting Colorado.
Suddenly, Hanging Lake—once hidden in the quiet
cove of Glenwood Canyon—was known by everyone.

Eventually, I wanted to introduce my then-boyfriend
(now-husband) to this treasure of my childhood.
I wanted him to behold those red, towering walls,
the sharp, slender footpath, and lustrous lake.
So we drove up I-70 into the lap of our great

Rocky Mountains; I was giddy to see my old friend,
and entirely unprepared for the scene that awaited us.

There were cars lined up all the way back to the highway
just to get into the newly expanded parking lot. The crowds
were enormous, but we had driven two hours, so decided to wait.
After a long while we found a spot, parked the car and walked
toward the trailhead where we joined a line of people slowly
inching their way toward the summit. There was trash on the ground,
music blaring from speakers, and yelling across the canyon.
I walked along in shock with that flippant procession;
sorrow and horror washing over me in waves.

But we carried on, as I wanted to show my love the spot we
stopped for picnics, and that clear blue water. When we arrived,
the footbridges were so crowded there was nowhere to sit,
and beer cans floated in the lake. My heart throbbed,
as if the offense had been inflicted upon my own body;
and surely it had. I could taste the gross disrespect
of each person swarming around with their cameras,
taking so much and leaving so little in its place.

In that moment I knew something, if ever so small,
of what the Native Peoples to these lands
must feel like when they look out across
all that has been done to their familial grounds.

SHOVELING PAIN

All that's been handed down to us,
we hand off to others. No one
considers grief to be an asset

in a story forever spinning
toward the future.

But if we look back
to see the setting sun,
with his peach and violet rays
fanning out across all
that has ever been,

we can behold heartbreak
as a kind of communion.

If not, we become
shells of ourselves,

shoveling pain into the
provenance of our bones.

When tears are not permitted
to flow, where do they go?

What dammed up reservoir
is being held hostage
inside of us?

MISCARRIAGES OF JUSTICE

If witch means wise woman,
then what happens when all the
wise women of the world are killed?

Don't be so quick to hand over an answer.

Mary MacLeod of Rodel was a Gaelic poet
who was buried face down under stones—
the puritanical way of tending to a witch,
so that her soul would be weighted forever.

She was killed for reciting poetry,
a subversive act for any woman
or admirer of decency.

Each time I stand on stage
my whole being shakes;
I relive the moments

where wisdom was misused
against the ones who upheld it.

And after the show is over? Well,
that's when the torment really begins.

I lay awake in bed, every inch of my body
burning. My cells endure their dread;
tens of thousands of European women—

so many, our ancestors—murdered
for being artists, seers, teachers,
healers, and memory keepers.

Even now, I feel terrified of being set aflame
or tortured to confess to something I did not do
(nor do I believe it would be wrong, if I had).

So I converse with my grandmothers and aunties
who are swimming in my blood. I tell them
about the times we are living in now—

how the church is not out to get me,
it has thoroughly forgotten my name.

This requires a lot of consolation
(words I'm not even sure I believe)
but they hold vigil deep into the night,
so my kinship is what I can offer.

Great, great, great granddaughters:
each time we stand, dance, or declare
some ligament of truth, we do so for them.

There is wisdom among us yet.

POETRY OF THE SACRED

Recently, a prompt
was foisted upon me:

write something eloquent
in regard to poetry
of the sacred.

So I stared at the wall.
Isn't everything
sacred?

Maybe then
I should write about

the wall.

It's always good
to be reminded why

one seldom solicits
prompts.

SENSELESS DEATHS

I grew up in Littleton, Colorado—a fairly unremarkable,
white suburban enclave. I was in middle school,
only a few miles away from Columbine, when the shooting
broke out. We were put on lockdown for several hours,
trembling in the little seats of our cream colored desks.

It was the day after my thirteenth birthday,
April 20th, 1999, which is also when Taurus begins
on the zodiac calendar, as well as the day of Hitler's birth—
speculated by some, to be the shooters' motivation.

One of my friend's brothers was killed
and a girl I took ballet with was trapped
in the dreaded library, where ten other
teenagers endured their final breaths.

It took a long time for her to return to the studio
but when she did, her body was stiff—frozen in time.
For the second year in a row, she and I were cast as soldiers
in the Nutcracker, but she eventually backed out because her hands
would not wrap themselves around those long, wooden guns.

When I tell someone where I am from, I watch as recognition,
mixed with something akin to pity or condolence, unfurls
across their well-meaning face. I often forget what our little town

is now known for, as I ready myself to explain where it is
and how they've probably never heard of it before.
What a sorrowful way of gaining recognition.

And the two teenage boys (whom I will not name)
also became famous; all pent up with rage and access
to far too many guns. No cultural inheritance or people
to call their own; using their violent actions and the
senseless deaths of others to ensure that their names
would get written down in the history books.

Certainly, this bloody outcry for attention
is fed by all the curious eyes feasting upon
their faces and tragic lives. But does
anyone know the names of the
thirteen others that were killed?

Does anyone care about their stories,
or what they dreamt of each night?
I lay awake wondering, still.

WHAT IS LOST

Goddesses know our names
by the architecture of our tears.

Life hangs in the balance
between rupture and prayer.

We are so quick
to hand our spirits over
to indignation,

but I want to know what is lost
in this landscape of light.

We ready ourselves
for things that may never come,
but what arrives faithfully
and with little fanfare,

we are often
so ill-prepared.

The hallowed ones,
they do not fall prey to deception—
their eyes were made to burn holes
into the backs of treacherous bandits
from miles and miles away.

Fortify your hearts, they tell us.
Apprentice to all that you cannot see.

I am angered often,
but tonight
I weep.

THE GODS' GARDEN

Your dad recently died
and your stepmom was already
dating someone else—
you were awash in heartbreak.

So we walked
those thin, red trails
in heartbreak.

We wondered about things—
love, grief, the history of inheritance.
We spoke in the presence of Gods,

not as if one day they might overhear
our words lifted skyward, but as though
we were surrounded by them there and then;

our willingness to be human
fed the unfolding breadth
of their mythic lives.

We never considered our place
within creation to be insignificant,
that if we retreated for awhile
no one would notice.

It's as if you were asking me
to rewrite the story, to not preserve
that same strand of madness.

You believed you were incapable,
yet somehow I would be granted the ability
to do and say all of the things
I had never seen or heard.

I don't always feel courageous,
but this is my way of proceeding as if
all of the world was built upon
this one, humble promise.

FIELD GUIDES FOR LIBERATION

Today, in Burma, there are poets
being killed and imprisoned.

Read that sentence again.

I have read it several times
and still it barely sinks in.

What is so threatening
about the poet?

To any society bent on control
and greed, surely artists represent
the most untamable breed,

but poets wield language
as an alchemical force;

words and stories that get lodged
into our imaginations, quietly crafting
field guides for our liberation.

Maung Yu Py faces two years in prison
after being severely beaten for his poetry.
I have read the English translation
of his piece Under The Great Ice Sheet,
and it is pure beauty latched to the breast of truth.
It's something I wish every beating heart

could read or hear spoken aloud
with the dawning sun.

In my early twenties I spent some time in Thailand
and while there lent a hand at a school for Burmese refugees;
they wanted someone to teach the children English.
I knew nothing of Burmese (not to mention,
very little of English) even so, my answer was yes.

We huddled together in a one-room, makeshift schoolhouse
with brightly painted walls—sitting on the floor and sweating
in that humid, December air. There were never enough pencils
to go around, but still, we spent our days in the company

of wonder and words.
The children were all ages;
peering at me behind poets' eyes.

I have read about another Burmese writer
who spent six years in solitary confinement,
and when she was released, she kept on writing.

Today, I write alongside them.

BURNT SIENNA

As a little girl, I loved my grandfather's art desk;
I had never seen anything so well organized
or overburdened by inspiration. I would sit in front of it
while he would sit in front of his easel; each quietly
marveling at the Mystery set out before us.

His brushes of various sizes and shapes
were always elegantly displayed
like long stem roses in vases or mugs
that my grandmother had made—
scattered about on the desk,
bearing visions of whatever canvas
they last touched. Then, there were all
the bottles, bowls, boxes, and drawers,
each adorned with their own label
in my grandfather's careful handwriting.
I loved sifting through those valleys of treasure—
slumbering charcoal, piles of paints and gloss,
perfectly sharpened pencils, erasers, and
newspaper clippings of things he had
already sketched or was hoping to return to—
pictures of horses, mountains, and Miles Davis.

He collected wooden cigar boxes for his watercolors,
which he would clean out, then line the inside with
splotched up paper to display the names of the sundry

hues contained within. I now have one of these boxes,
so old and plainly handsome. The wood is weathered
through years of devout use and there is a delicate,
antique brass latch that still fastens shut. The crest
on the top says, "J-R Special Coronas No. 2."

I use this piece of patrimony as a jewelry box;
inside, a clutter of handmade bracelets, and on the lid
there are still the circles containing names and
blotches of each of his beloved colors.

Sepia, Sap Green, Cadmium Red,
Vermillion, Violet, Burnt Sienna, Cobalt,
Indigo, Pale Orange, Deer Yellow.

I look at his scripted penmanship,
then at his paintings hung all over
the walls of our workshop,
and wonder which color he chose
for that trumpet, this tree, those lips.

My grandfather was not a stranger to heartache,
though he committed his days to bringing beauty
back into his cherished corner of the world.

FREIGHTS OF LIGHT

The Old Ones live on in the eyes of the young,
and the young carry them along studiously.

Together, they look out across all the colors
and slanting shoulders of creation;
they pen verse inside those
big bowls of delight.

When I look into my dad's kind eyes,
I see my grandmother's—

almond shaped,
all affection and pride.

When my dad looks into my eyes,
he sees his mother's—

warm, unflinching
freights of light.

We share her
through these great pools
of love and longing,

lifting up the sky.

I WILL BREATHE FOR YOU

When you cannot breathe,
I will breathe for you.

When you are bound inside,
unable to taste the fervent air
or feel the bottoms of your feet
held holy by the ground,

I will go out and
lay this body down.

When the tears refuse to come,
I will dump buckets atop the Earth—

I will pray for the Gods
to lift you on their backs,

to carry your name
through this undercurrent
of night. I will be waiting

with handwoven
baskets and belts,

a profusion of wild flowers,
and a body made for listening.

I will shepherd your story
over to the other side.

HAND SPUN

For Myrna

Your tremors are seasoned by poetry—
a truthful, tenderized elegance
in the way your hands shake,
finding their way to all the things
they still love. How you dig into your closet
and crowded drawers to show me the
riches you have made over a lifetime,
one by one, carrying them like jewels
into the gray room—windows streaked with rain.

Your hands flutter like two hummingbirds
as they hold up each precious thing to be praised;
the petite bowl you carved out of wood
which cradles the dried fruit and nuts
you offer as our afternoon snack.

The basket of vibrantly woven hats
and scarves, all from yarn that you hand dyed,
and before that, hand spun from sheep
you helped to shear. The necklaces,
half-knit sweater, and all those other things
you could not find nor remember,
yet swore the better half of your time to.

And now, the tremors make intricate work
nearly impossible; but you still run your fingers
through piles of wool and remember
the rhythm of your crochet needle hooking
onto the next loop, then pulling under and
through the storied fibers of your days.

You sit patiently with me—positioned on the couch
as I scoot closer to your exquisite spinning wheel—
directing my steady hands in how to stretch and hold
and guide the soft pillows of white and gray
into fine strands of bountiful light.

I pray I am blessed with a long life, like you;
now eighty, surrounded by so much beauty
and a great-granddaughter on the way.

If I am lucky enough to become old and gray,
and if my hands stop following those elaborate
patterns of my youth, I promise to pave a way
for the young ones to fill in that emptied space.
I will clear out all of the shelves and drawers
to show them what a fine life is made from.

A WAKING DREAM

There is a footpath right outside our front door
which winds up the handsome and wildly
rugged mountain overlooking our house.

It wasn't so pronounced when we first moved here,
though for two years I have walked up and down,
tattooing a mark of devotion atop the merciful Earth.

Depending upon the season, I wind my way
around prickly pear cactus, wildflowers,
sage, the occasional snake, or snow.
It is a dream to wake into, over and again.

My feet are familiar with this terrain,
but even still, my eyes scan the ground;
finding places to step over and around
the sleeping rocks covered by moss.

One morning, I spot a soft, white and gray feather
resting at the boot tips of a thick pine tree. I bow down
to pick it up, marveling at the shape and lightness of character;
turning it round and round in my sun hardened hands.

Suddenly I sense someone standing above me,
so I slowly lift my eyes to the first few branches
three feet above my head. There sit two bundles of fluff,
huddled in close to one another and staring at me behind wide,
blinking eyes. Baby great horned owls, all full of curiosity
and fright. *Who is this strange two-legged creature?*
they inquire, as their tiny hearts pound
into the plum of their chests.

I immediately drop to my knees, in reverence
or rapture, and introduce myself as the one
who lives just down the mountain.

We stay like that for a long while,
staring across the great divide
into one another's eyes.

If ever I go missing,
you will find me there—
kneeling, still.

WILD TURKEYS

Is all of life full of laughter
and plumage?

Perhaps I've gotten the story wrong:
pain, if tended to properly,
can plummet into joy.

So I leave behind
what society

has bestowed upon me.

Strength is a bird
that lives in one's bones;
it is memory. And pain—

well, that's memory too.

HEADWATERS OF THE SOUL

We are all pilgrims of the heart,
walking toward or away from
the headwaters of our souls.

What we know
is so very little,

though we pretend
at so much more.

But there go the spring rains again
with their bias for blessing—

ladybugs in the lettuce,
new blossoms alight
on the fingertips
of every warbling tree.

And that dark maiden
waking from her winter slumber
deep within the Earth,

pushing her soiled limbs
and legends upward
through our own buzzing
bodie—now re-rooted
into the fertile webbing
of all that we cannot see.

ICH LIEBE DICH

How easy it is to keep myself
from missing you;

your hands with their purple veins
running through the province
of rivers and time.

The way they guided fabric
so smoothly through the shining foot
of your old sewing machine—
making elaborate gifts
for every person you ever met.

The way you said my name
always with an "e" at the end,
like a lullaby or curtsy
to finish class.

That time you came with me
to campus, for our made-up
take-your-mother-to-school-day;

you, having never attended college,
sat wide-eyed in each room
drinking in the wine of novelty
and knowledge.

How you swore by the importance of tasting
one cookie from every batch you pulled out
of the oven, if purely to know something
of the sweetness you intended for others.

When you wanted to recreate the infused vodka
you so adored drinking on the streets of Germany,
we spent hours squeezing lemons in your kitchen—
our hands were swollen from the juices,
we laughed so hard we cried.

That day in the hospital we folded over
Rilke's original German verse as though
studying scripture—and surely we were.

How you helped me translate
the lines into English, remembering
words spoken around your grandparents
kitchen, or while out in the garden;
knowing that nouns were capitalized
from the few courses you took
way back in high school.

We spent hours tracing the hallowed language
of our people; sitting on hard chairs by the window
with the lights turned off as the fluorescents hurt

your eyes. And when the nurse poked her head in
to see if we were alright, you smiled kindly at her,
as you always did, even through pain and exhaustion.

I imagine our ancestors gathered round
the glass from outside, pressing their ears
against the gleaming surface to listen
for the words they had grown to miss.

Ich liebe dich was the first phrase
you taught me, the opening to poem
I, 25 in the Book of Hours.

We chanted it over and again,
in pure exultation.

Ich liebe dich. I love you.
Ich liebe dich. I love you.

Ich liebe dich, Mutter.
I love you, Mother.

I truly do.

CONTINUING ON

First crocus of spring—little purple,
fuzzy love, unfolding into light.
I kneel down to praise you

when suddenly, our silly dog
full of reckless revelry

comes bounding up
to wrap his long snout
around your soft head.

I am aghast. *No!*
Not the very first flower
bravely pushing herself past
the kingdom of winter.

But when he runs off,
I see the little bud
has slid through
his jagged teeth

and is miraculously
still standing—

a bit of slobber on her petals
now gleaming in the sun.

Isn't life like that?

Some unforeseen creature
comes swooping in

to gnaw
our heads off,

yet somehow we manage
(though, slightly mangled)

to continue on
into the goodness
of the day.

IN THE ABSENCE OF CONSENT

Recently, an early draft of Allen Ginsberg's
renowned poem, Howl, was found
and is now on a freight train to publication.
The carbon copy is being auctioned off
for a half million dollars. People claim
this is an important part of understanding
the poet's mind as he worked on the final version.

Has anyone considered that it might be intrusive
to pry inside of a person's mind; that he
edited out those lines for a particular reason?

How Mr. Ginsberg could be rolling over in his grave
to know that intimate and unwrought thoughts
are now being analyzed and peddled for profit?

This is the moment when edges blur
between celebrity and humanity—
when our emptiness turns grotesque.

It is also my worst nightmare,
to imagine anyone ransacking
my journals after I am dead;

those disorganized tendrils of thought
being born in patient sanctuaries
free from need or explanation.

So once I fill every page of any bound book
(which often takes years) I feed them to the fire,
one slow morale at a time, like a thousand course meal.
My writer friends call this audacious; I detect horror
in their eyes. But how can one expect more poetry
to pour forth from any Muse with all those words
hoarded away, collecting dust on the top shelf?

SPELL CASTING

It is now week two in the trial
for George Floyd's murder—
unfathomable things happen
every day, and this is one of them.

I heard on the radio that the defense is cowering
behind the story of a drug overdose;
that this was the reason an innocent Black man
died in the street, not the nine minutes
a white police officer spent kneeling on his neck.

I am an abiding believer in stories
and language; words cast spells—
they create the world in which we live.

To float such a twisted narrative
into the minds of millions of listeners
is an absurdly dangerous thing.

I'd like to meet the person
who first thought up this idea,
and the others sitting in the room
around him, nodding their heads
in agreement to such perversion

of speech. I'd like to ask them
how well they sleep.

I'm now on night five of no sleep,
and while clearly no saint, I do my best
not to lie or cause needless harm to others.

Sleep deprivation was used as a torture technique
in Medieval Europe to get women to confess
to witchcraft—it creates hallucinations
and brings a person past the brink of sanity.
At only five days in, I can already see
how that kind of rough road gets paved.

But what about those who sleep too well
when their lies are lighting others aflame?

Does their torture get deferred?
If so, to whom, and when?

HAVING TEARS AT ALL

Nothing really matters.
Or, wait—is it everything
fully matters? Yes,
that is the one.

This lemon daffodil,
that lapping fog.

These children chanting
praise hymns over here,
those kids sewing your clothes
in dreadful factories over there.

This leaf, that language—
lifted kite, sleepless night.

The streaks that tears make
down your dry, or round, or
wrinkled face; the sanctity
of water, of having tears at all.

Boredom, admiration,
barely making it by.

His tenderness,
her intuition,
their truth;

our past,
the uncertain future
of our young,

and every song
yet to be sung.

MR. MONTMORENCY

Last year, my dad gave us a cherry tree
as a housewarming gift; he calls
every so often to see how it's doing.

"Is he getting enough water?" my dad asks.
I say yes, though never can be sure; but he does
seem happy enough standing there beside the raspberries.

"You know, sweetie, the first year is the hardest to get through,"
my dad says. "If he can make it past this, he'll live through
anything." I think how accurate that is of grief, too.

Today he calls to say that he has some rose bushes
to give us, both yellow and red; then tells me how much
water they'll need, and that they prefer full sun.

"I bet they'd like to be beside your front door,"
he says, as though he's been thinking about it
a long while. "But I'll come over and take a look
around, we'll find the right place for them."

I think of this good man, born in Brooklyn
with concrete all around—who loves bushes,
trees, and flowers. Who spends a large part
of most days digging holes, then placing roots
into the opened soil, covering them up again,
and standing back in admiration.

Maybe the formative years of our lives
reveal to us what the world is lacking,
and how it is we are each meant
to fill in that emptied space.

SOMETHING MORE

Too tired to think of change,
you think about food—

the tastes and textures
from your childhood
and centuries before,

now replaced
by predictability;

by something in a box,
which bears no resemblance
to the shape of your ancestors
bent over the land,

pressing their songs and seeds
into the reciprocal Earth.

Nor their way of wandering
the woods, trailing the breath
of all the life that ever loved them.

So you eat and eat
but satisfaction never comes,
even as the box promises pleasure.

Perhaps pleasure is not the thing
you are after, though it's been dressed up
in shiny clothes and sold back to us
as religion. There is a slow

and ever present
drumbeat in your belly—
it carries the memory
of something more.

BETWEEN THE STARS

Homesickness is the temple you circle round,
like a turkey vulture scanning the prairie for food.
The mouse sees the vulture soaring—
counts each orbit as he fingers
the rosary of his last remaining days.

The only sanctity is time,
such a tender thing—

giving up the life
you carefully planned

to fall, heart first,
into another.

Your soul
is leading now;

your story is being thrust
back and forth
between the stars.

It is our story.
I am yours.

THE BALLAD OF MY DREAMS

All day long you listen to my heart beating—
to our muffled voices and prayers
pouring through the constellation of cells
that now parent the song-lines of your life.

At night, do you bathe
in the ballad of my dreaming,
or am I bathing in yours?

Fierce and future cub,
held within your grandma's
oceanic embrace—

I long to look into your eyes,
to know your storied name.

I long to place you
in your grandpa's arms,

to show his wary bones
that although they tried
to exterminate us,

we are still
so wholly here.

IT COULD ALSO BE TRUE

Maybe all poetry is memory—
maybe it drips from the unborn tears
of our parents, and their parents, and theirs?

And if that is true,
then it could also
be true

that anything remembered
is the embodiment of poetics,

no matter how painful or maddening;
how meager or grandiose.

That we might count our fortunes
based on how we are gathered
into the hands of something so fleeting,
so shy in its desire for affection.

On occasion, the world will asks us
to pause for a time, to taste again
the visions of our lives

so seldom afforded the breadth
they extend in return.

On that day, will you stand or kneel
with your broken open heart
facing outward to the cosmos—

will you become a thing worth
remembering; and in that way

remember, too?

ABOUT THE AUTHOR

April Tierney lives in the foothills of the Colorado Rocky Mountains with her husband, young daughter, mischievous dog, and wide web of kin. She is the author of three full length collections of poetry, as well as the co-author of a chapbook and photographic anthology. Her writing has been featured in *The Wayfarer Magazine*, *Orion*, and *Real Ground Journal*, among other publications.

Learn more at apriltierney.com.

WAYFARER

BASED IN THE BERKSHIRE MOUNTAINS, MASS.

The Wayfarer Magazine. Since 2012, *The Wayfarer* has been offering literature, interviews, and art with the intention to inspires our readers, enrich their lives, and highlight the power for agency and change-making that each individual holds. By our definition, a wayfarer is one whose inner-compass is ever-oriented to truth, wisdom, healing, and beauty in their own wandering. The Wayfarer's mission as a publication is to foster a community of contemplative voices and provide readers with resources and perspectives that support them in their own journey.

Wayfarer Books is our newest imprint! After nearly 10 years in print, *The Wayfarer Magazine* is branching out from our magazine to become a full-fledged publishing house offering full-length works of eco-literature!

Wayfarer Farm & Retreat is our latest endeavor, springing up the Berkshire Mountains of Massachusetts. Set to open to the public in 2024, the 15 acre retreat will offer workshops, farm-to-table dinners, off-grid retreat cabins, and artist residencies.

WWW.WAYFARERBOOKS.ORG